Going Places

IN A C

By Robert M. Hamilton

Gareth Stevens
Publishing

Please visit our website, www.garethstevens.com. For a free color catalog of all our high-quality books, call toll free 1-800-542-2595 or fax 1-877-542-2596.

Library of Congress Cataloging-in-Publication Data

Hamilton, Robert M., 1987-
In a car / Robert M. Hamilton.
    p. cm.— (Going places)
Includes index.
ISBN 978-1-4339-6263-9 (pbk.)
ISBN 978-1-4339-6264-6 (6-pack)
ISBN 978-1-4339-6261-5 (lib. bdg.)
1. Automobiles—Juvenile literature. 2. Automobile travel—Juvenile literature. I. Title.
TL206.H36 2012
388.3'21—dc23
                                    2011030078

First Edition

Published in 2012 by
Gareth Stevens Publishing
111 East 14th Street, Suite 349
New York, NY 10003

Copyright © 2012 Gareth Stevens Publishing

Editor: Katie Kawa
Designer: Andrea Davison-Bartolotta

Photo credits: Cover Noel Handerickson/Digital Vision/Thinkstock; p. 1 Stephen Mcsweeny/Shutterstock.com; pp. 5, 9, 13, 19, 23, 24 (pedal) Shutterstock.com; p. 7 Adrian Coroama/Shutterstock.com; p. 11 iStockphoto/Thinkstock; pp. 15, 24 (steering wheel) Jupiterimages/Creatas/Thinkstock; p. 17 Jupiterimages/Polka Dot/Thinkstock; p. 21 Elena Elisseeva/Shutterstock.com; p. 24 (gasoline) iStockphoto.com.

Printed in the United States of America

CPSIA compliance information: Batch #CW12GS: For further information contact Gareth Stevens, New York, New York at 1-800-542-2595.

Contents

A car moves
on four wheels.

Tires cover the wheels.
They are made
of rubber.

A car has two pedals.
People push them
with their feet.

9

One pedal is the gas.
It makes the car go.

One is the brake.
It makes the car stop.

13

A car has
a steering wheel.
This turns the car.

15

A person turns the key.
Then, the car can go.

A car needs gasoline to make it go. It comes from a gas station.

19

Many people drive cars.
They can go fast!

There are rules for how fast cars can go. They are called speed limits.

23

Words to Know

gasoline   pedal   steering wheel

Index